PETS PLUS

Lizards and Snakes

Sally Morgan

Smart Apple Media

Published by Smart Apple Media, an imprint of Black Rabbit Books
P.O. Box 3263, Mankato, Minnesota 56002
www.blackrabbitbooks.com

Printed in the United States of America at Corporate Graphics, Inc. North Mankato, Minnesota.

Published by arrangement with the Watts Publishing Group LTD, London.

Library of Congress Cataloging-in-Publication Data
Morgan, Sally, 1957-
  Lizards and snakes / Sally Morgan.
    p. cm. -- (Pets plus) > Includes index.
  ISBN 978-1-59920-704-9 (library binding)
  1. Lizards--Juvenile literature. 2. Snakes--Juvenile literature. I. Title.
  QL666.L2M64 2012
  597.95--dc23
                        2011025317

Created by Taglines Creative Ltd: www.taglinescreative.com
Author: Sally Morgan
Series designer: Hayley Cove
Editor: Jean Coppendale

Picture credits
t=top b=bottom l=left r=right m=middle
Cover: Grass snake, Shutterstock/Miroslav Hlavko; Skink, Shutterstock/Angel Simon; green anole lizard,
Shutterstock/Leigh Prather; snake skin, Shutterstock/Mars Evis; Title page: lizards, Shutterstock/Cathy
Keifer; rattlesnake, Papilio/Robert Pickett; Contents and top of spreads: ball python, Shutterstock/
Fivespots; bearded dragon, Shutterstoc/Eric Isselee; p4 Shutterstock/Anna Lafrentz;
p5 both Shutterstock/Eric Isselee; p6 Alamy/Blickwinkel; p7 Alamy/Acestock;
p7 Do it Shutterstock/ Fivespots; p8t Shutterstock/Fivespots, 18b Alamy/Paul Doyle;
p9 Alamy/Juniors Bildarchiv; p10 Alamy/Juniors Bildarchiv; p11 Ecoscene/Vicki
Coombs; p12 Alamy/Juniors Bildarchiv; p13 Shutterstock/Julie Keen;
p14 Alamy/Chris Mattison; p15l Shutterstock/Insuratelu Gabriela Gianina,
15r Ecoscene/Sally Morgan; p16 Ecoscene/Robert Pickett; p17 Shutterstock/
Alexander Chaikin; p18 Ardea/ Duncan Usher; p19t Alan Towse/
Ecoscene, p19bl Shutterstock Borhuah Chen, 19bm Borhuah
Chen, 19br Rusty Dodson; p20 Shutterstock/Joel Kempson;
p21l Shutterstock/Uzunova, 21r Alamy Yvette Cardozo;
p22t Shutterstock/PPL, 22r Shutterstock/Tratong,
p23 Shutterstock/Sergey Goruppa; p24 Shutterstock/
Cathy Keifer; p25tShutterstock Bob Blanchard,
25b Shutterstock/Istomina Olena; p26 Reinhard Dirscherl/
Ecoscene; p27t Shutterstock/ Fivespots, 27b Shutterstock/
BMCL; p29t Shutterstock/Insuratelu Gabriela Gianina,
29b Vicki Coombs/Ecoscene; p30 snake Shutterstock/
Miroslav Hlavko; p31 Shutterstock/ Angel Simon;
p32 Shutterstock/Eric Isselee

Every attempt has been made to clear copyright.
Should there be any inadvertent omission please
apply to the publisher for rectification.

PO 1594 / Mar 2013

9 8 7 6 5 4 3

Contents

The meaning of the words in **bold** can be found in the glossary on pages 30–31.

Reptiles—Exotic Pets

Lizards and snakes are reptiles. Together with animals such as spiders, scorpions, and turtles they are called **exotic** pets.

What Is a Reptile?

Reptiles are animals that have a backbone. They also have a scaly skin and lay eggs. Reptiles such as crocodiles and turtles have four legs, as do most lizards. However, snakes and slow worms (a type of lizard) are legless. They use their long body to slither across the ground. Skinks are lizards with a long body and four legs.

▼ A skink is a good choice for a first pet lizard.

▲ In the wild, corn snakes are brown and orange with dark brown bands (left) but some pet corn snakes are white (right).

Wild or Pet

Pet lizards and snakes behave in the same way as wild lizards and snakes, but some pet snakes may look different from the wild **species**. This is because snakes that have been bred in **captivity** can be colors that are not found in the wild. For example, there are white and gold corn snakes and **albino** ball pythons.

Think Before You Buy

Lizards and snakes are not easy pets to keep. They need a lot of care and special equipment. It is important to learn how to care for these animals before you buy one. Remember that a small, young snake will grow into a large animal.

PET POINT
Some lizards and snakes have to be fed live food. Do you have a local supplier?

Why a Lizard or Snake?

Lizards and snakes are fascinating animals. They don't have to be walked or groomed, but they do need to be checked every day.

Buying Your Pet

You can buy a pet snake or lizard from a specialist pet shop or from a **breeder**. Before you buy, visit the shop or breeder. Make sure they keep the animals clean and that the animals look healthy. The person you buy your pet from should be able to help you buy the right size tank.

PET POINT

Larger snakes need a big tank so the housing costs are more expensive.

▼ A shop that sells reptiles should also sell you the equipment you need.

Captive Bred, Not Wild

It is very important to ask if the animal was bred in captivity. Many exotic snakes and lizards are caught in the wild and sold as pets. This trade is threatening the survival of the animals in the wild. A **captive bred** animal will be used to people and will be much easier to handle.

▼ Choose a snake that is alert and curious and, like this python, gently grips your hand or arm when it is handled.

Do It!

Look out for these words when you buy a snake or lizard

- Wild Caught or Wild Collected (WC)—this means the animal was caught in the wild
- Captive Farmed (CF)—the animal was bred in captivity, often on a farm, in its country of origin
- Captive Bred (CB) —the animal was bred in captivity in the country in which it is for sale

Snake or Lizard?

Snakes make better pets. Most are easy to handle and feed. Some of the smaller lizards, such as geckos, can be difficult to handle. Choose a lizard that doesn't like to bite – check this with your supplier. Many lizards have strong jaws that they use to crush their food, so they can pinch a finger quite hard.

Which Type?

Some snakes and lizards can grow large and heavy, while others are small. Some live for many years, others for only a few years.

Good Snake Choices

Don't buy venomous snakes, which are dangerous to keep. Choose easy care snakes such as the garter, corn, milk, or king snakes. Garter snakes are very active in the wild and in captivity. Some snakes are **nocturnal** and will sleep all day.

▲ Ball pythons grow to about 4.6–5 feet (1.4–1.5 m).

Pythons

A captive bred ball python is a good snake for a beginner as it is easy to handle and feed. This python gets its name from the way it rolls itself into a tight ball when it is threatened. Ball pythons are nocturnal, so you can't handle them during daylight. In the wild, they sleep hidden away during the day to avoid **predators**.

◄ Corn snakes enjoy being handled.

▲ The bearded dragon is a big active lizard, so it needs a large tank with an **ultraviolet light**.

Lizards for Beginners

Easy care lizards include the leopard gecko, blue-tongued skink, and the bearded dragon. These lizards enjoy being handled and are easy to care for and feed. Lizards that are active during the day need an ultraviolet light to stay healthy. This is because natural ultraviolet light cannot pass through glass.

PET POINT

Iguanas are popular lizards, but they grow large and can be **aggressive**. Only choose an iguana when you have some experience with lizards.

Preparing a New Home

Once you've made your choice of lizard or snake, you can prepare for its arrival. Set up its new home before you buy your pet.

Getting Ready

Reptiles are usually kept in a large glass or plastic tank. A snake needs to be able to stretch out and climb branches. For example, a corn snake can grow to 5 feet (1.5 m) in length so it needs a tank at least 3 feet (1.0 m) long, 1.3 feet (0.4 m) wide, and 1.3 feet (0.4 m) high.

Decorating Its Home

Add branches and bark logs to make your pet's tank more like a wild **habitat**. Remember snakes and lizards need space to move around, so don't add too much clutter. Most important is a place for your pet to hide, such as a hollow log or even a shoe box.

▲ In the wild, snakes and lizards have a lot of enemies, so a hiding place will make them feel safe even though they don't have any enemies in the tank.

Temperature Control

Wild lizards and snakes bask in the sun to warm up, and move into the shade to get cool. Your pet will need a heat source to keep its body at the right temperature. You can use an electric heating pad, which is placed either under or inside the tank. If the tank is too cool, your pet will sleep all day.

▼ You will need a small box or tank to carry your pet to its new home.

Do It!

Checklist: Things you will need for your new pet:

- tank with a secure lid
- heating pad and light
- thermometer to check the tank temperature
- bottom cover for the tank, such as newspaper or bark
- logs and branches, or pieces of cork bark to put in the tank
- water bowl
- food supply—ask the shop or breeder what your pet will eat
- box to transport the animal home

Caring for Your Pet

Snakes and lizards need plenty of care. Some things, like providing fresh water, need to be done daily. Other things can be done less often.

Regular Care

Daily jobs include checking the tank temperature, providing fresh drinking water, and removing the animal's droppings. Every month you need to remove your pet to give the tank a good clean—wash down the glass and the floor with soapy water.

> ## Do It!
>
> Lizards and snakes can carry **bacteria** that can make you sick, so always wash your hands after handling your pet or touching its tank.

▼ This bearded dragon has a clean tank and a large bowl of fresh water.

Fresh Water

Make sure your pet has clean water every day. Some snakes like to soak in water, so they need a bowl large enough to do this. Many geckos live in a **humid climate**, so pet geckos like the insides of their tank to be sprayed with a fine mist of water. Then they can sip the water droplets as they would do in the wild, rather than drink from a bowl.

▲ This iguana is being treated by a vet.

Is Something Wrong?

If you spend time with your pet, you will know when something is wrong. Perhaps it is not eating or not moving much. It may be breathing heavily, have foam around its mouth, or have runny eyes. If you think your pet is sick, take it to a vet who treats exotic pets.

PET POINT

Don't keep on lifting up logs and bark to look at your pet. They like to be left alone, so respect their space.

Handling Your Pet

Snakes and lizards that are captive bred are used to being picked up and handled from the moment they are born.

Wriggling Snakes

Even captive bred snakes may be tricky to handle at first, so don't be upset if your pet wriggles or nibbles your hand. Do everything slowly when handling your pet and be quiet—it will soon get used to you. Fast movements will make your snake think you are a predator and will scare it.

▼ All pet snakes, such as this milk snake, should be held firmly but gently—do not squeeze your pet.

PET POINT

When you first pick up a snake it may poop or produce a smelly liquid called **musk** because it is scared. Don't drop them when they do this!

Handling Lizards

Many lizards do not like being handled, so don't bother them unless it's necessary. To move lizards to clean their tank, scoop them up in your hand. Gently hold one front leg so they cannot escape, or catch them in a canvas bag or a box. Some lizards enjoy being handled. The bearded dragon will enjoy sitting on your arm or shoulder.

Toes and Tails

Young lizards are small and their tiny fingers and toes are easily injured if you are rough when you handle them. Don't hold them close to your mouth as they may think you are going to eat them and get very stressed. Many lizards lose their tail if they are threatened. This is something that they do in the wild to escape from predators.

◀ This skink is being held in the right way—never grab your lizard by the tail in case it comes off.

▼ This agama lizard has lost its tail and grown a new one, but it does not look the same as the original tail.

Wild Cousins

The way your pet lizard or snake behaves is very similar to the way snakes and lizards behave in the wild.

Nocturnal

Many snakes are nocturnal. In the wild they stay hidden during the day, and come out at night to hunt for food. They have senses that allow them to detect the warm bodies of their **prey** in the dark. Your pet snake may sleep all day and be active at night, too.

▶ A rattlesnake in the wild looks for food at night.

Do Not Disturb

If your pet is one that is nocturnal in the wild, then let it sleep during the day. It will not like being pulled out of its hiding place to be handled. It will come out when it is dark to move around and feed.

Living in Trees

Many types of lizards and snakes are **arboreal**, which means that they spend most, or all, of their time in trees. These species include iguanas, geckos, boas, and pythons. They feed on other animals that live in the trees.

▲ In the wild, a gecko runs up and down trees in search of food.

PET POINT

Arboreal pet snakes need sturdy branches inside their tank so they can climb. Make sure any lights inside the tank are covered as the snake could climb over them and be burned.

Winter Sleep

Snakes living in cooler parts of the world, such as North America and Europe, survive the cold winter by slithering into a hole or a hollow tree trunk where they remain inactive. They sleep for most of the time and do not feed. This is called **brumation**. They come out in spring when the days are warmer. If the temperature in your tank is too low, your pet snake may begin to go into brumation.

Giving Birth

 If you keep a pair of lizards or snakes you may be very lucky. They may lay some eggs or give birth to young.

Eggs

Lizard or snake eggs are leathery, not hard like a chicken egg. Some eggs are oval or oblong, but others are just a strange lumpy shape. Most snakes lay their eggs underground in soil or sand, and then leave them. However, some snakes, such as cobras and pythons, guard their eggs.

Live Birth

Some lizards and snakes such as copperheads, boa **constrictors**, rattle snakes, and garter snakes do not lay eggs. Instead, the females give birth to live young. The young remain inside the body of their mother until they are large enough to survive on their own.

▲ This young common lizard looks just like the adult but is much smaller. These lizards do not hatch from an egg but are born live.

Molting

As lizards and snakes grow, their scales stop their skin from stretching. This means that as they get bigger, their skin becomes too tight. When this happens, they have to **shed** their old skin and grow a new, larger one. This is called **molting**.

▲ The old skin of the snake becomes loose so the snake can wriggle out.

Prepare for a Molt

Your pet will molt regularly. Before they start to molt, a snake stops eating, its skin becomes dull, and its eyes cloud over. Then it sheds its skin in one piece over 7 to 14 days. The skin of the lizard peels off in bits. Snakes can get a bit irritable when they are about to molt so it's best to leave them alone at this time.

Life Cycle

The life cycle of a king snake starts with the egg, which hatches after 40–65 days. A king snake is ready to breed when it is one or two years old. Wild king snakes live for about 20 years. A pet king snake can live for up to 30 years.

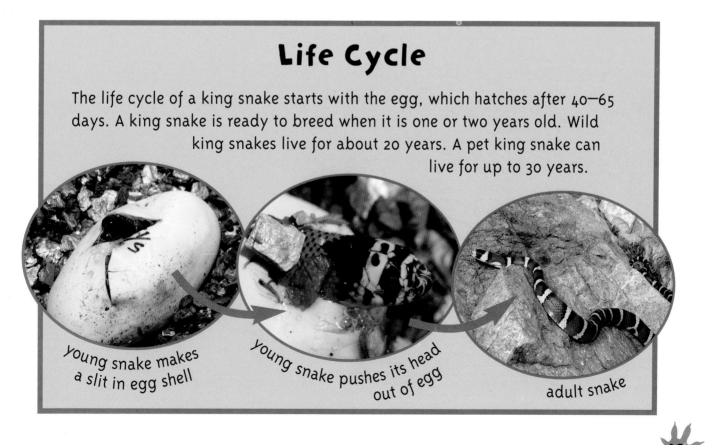

young snake makes a slit in egg shell

young snake pushes its head out of egg

adult snake

Hunting and Feeding

Lizards and snakes are predators—animals that hunt other animals for food. They catch their prey in many different ways.

Swallowed Whole

Snakes do not chew their food. Instead they swallow it whole, even if it is much larger than themselves. This is possible because they can **dislocate** their lower jaw so their mouth can open wide. Once the prey has been swallowed, the snake opens its mouth wide again to reconnect its jaws.

Feeding Your Snake

Pet snakes are usually fed dead mice and rats that are prefrozen. The mouse or rat is **defrosted** and placed on a dish for the snake to find. Young snakes are fed baby mice and rats, and they need one every few days. As snakes get older and larger, they can be fed adult mice and then rats.

▼ A pet corn snake will swallow its food whole, just like wild snakes.

▲ Lizards in the wild (left) keep very still as they watch for small animals to move. They then pounce on their prey. This pet lizard (right) watches live meal worms on a plate before snatching them up to eat.

Feeding Your Lizard

Many smaller lizards feed on animals such as crickets, grasshoppers, meal worms, and earthworms. You will have to place live ones in the tank every day because lizards like to see their prey move before they eat it. Larger lizards may eat prefrozen mice. A few, such as the green iguana, will eat fruits, vegetables, and flowers.

PET POINT

Snakes do not have to be fed every day. Check out feeding rules with your pet supplier. Do not handle your snake for a few days after feeding it as it may **regurgitate** its food.

Your Wild Pet

 Pet snakes and lizards behave in the same way as their wild cousins. If you are lucky, you can see these behavior patterns in your pet.

Enjoying the Heat

Your pet probably has a heating pad or other heat source in its tank. Wild lizards and snakes get their heat from the sun. In the morning, many lizards lie on rocks and bask in the sunlight to get warm.

Living Underground

In the wild, some snakes burrow underground to keep away from the sunlight or predators. Pet milk snakes like to burrow too, so they need a deep layer of wood shavings covering the floor of their tank.

▲ These pet iguanas (top) sit on rocks warmed by a special heating pad. A wild iguana (right) basks in sunlight.

Warnings

Some lizards, such as iguanas, use body language to warn other iguanas to stay away. When they are angry, their eyes open wide, their tail twitches, and their throat flap is pushed out. The same is true for pet iguanas. If you see one behaving like this, you know it's angry and you need to move away or it may **lunge** forward and bite.

Guarding Their Home

Many lizards are **territorial** in the wild. This means that they guard the area where they live and fight other lizards if they come too close. This is why you can only keep one male of some types of lizard, such as anole lizards. The pet shop or breeder should tell you which lizards should be kept alone.

▼ This angry iguana opens its eyes wide and pushes out its throat flap to make itself look big and scary.

23

Lizard Talk

Lizards can make a wide range of sounds, from clicks and chirps to barks, grunts, and squeals.

Noisy Geckos

Geckos are the most talkative lizards, especially the tokay geckos. Geckos come out at night and make loud barking sounds. They make these sounds to attract mates and to startle predators.

Body Talk

Lizards communicate in other ways, not just with sound. They bob their head up and down in front of each other, and swish their tails from side to side. This usually means they want to fight.

▲ Leopard geckos communicate using sounds, such as chirps, squeaks, and grunts.

▲ Anole lizards flash their brightly colored **dewlap** to startle predators and attract a female.

Bigger and Bigger

Lizards can raise their head crests and expand the dewlaps under their chin to make themselves look big. They do this to show off in front of other males or to frighten off enemies. Some pet geckos make a crackling sound if they do not want to be picked up, and wag their tail when they are excited.

Do It!

Mirror Talk

Pet lizards **display** just like their wild cousins. Put a mirror in their tank and watch how they behave in front of it. They will think it's another lizard and do a display, such as bobbing their head, doing push-ups, and lashing their tail.

Instant Expert

There are about 2,500 different species of snake and 2,200 types of lizard in the world, and more are found every year.

Large...

The largest living snake is the Indian python that reaches 29.5 ft. (9 m) in length and weighs a massive 250 lb. (113 kg). Another giant is the anaconda, which also grows to about 29.5 ft. (9 m). The anaconda is an amazing swimmer and is found in tropical swamps and rivers of the Amazon. The largest venomous snake is the king cobra that grows to about 18 ft. (5.5 m) in length.

The largest lizard is the Komodo dragon, which can weigh about 366 lb. (166 kg).

...and Small

The world's smallest snake is the Barbados thread snake. It has the Latin name *Leptotyphlops carlae* and was discovered on the island of Barbados in the Caribbean in 2008. It is just 4 in. (10 cm) long and looks like a piece of spaghetti.

The smallest lizard, *Sphaerodactylus ariasae,* is a type of dwarf gecko. It is 0.4 in. (16 mm) long and was found in 2001 on another Caribbean island.

◀ A huge Komodo dragon on the Island of Komodo in Indonesia.

Most Dangerous

The snakes that produce the most lethal **venom** are taipans, the Australian brown snakes, and sea snakes. A single bite from the Inland taipan contains enough venom to kill 100 adults. Luckily these snakes live in remote areas, so very few people are killed by them.

▲ The Inland taipan snake has a deadly bite.

Snake Bites

Around the world as many as 94,000 people are killed by snakes each year, the largest numbers occurring in South Asia, Southeast Asia, and Africa. The top four killer snakes are the Sri Lankan Russell's viper, Indian cobra, saw-scaled viper, and the common krait.

Pet Quiz

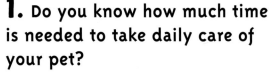

Now that you know a bit more about what is involved in looking after snakes and lizards, is a snake or lizard the right pet for you?

1. Do you know how much time is needed to take daily care of your pet?
- **a)** Not sure
- **b)** I don't have any time to look after it
- **c)** An hour a day

2. Is it important that you play with your pet?
- **a)** Yes, very important
- **b)** Somewhat important
- **c)** Not important

3. How much space do you need for a tank to house a snake or lizard?
- **a)** Not much
- **b)** Don't know
- **c)** Quite a lot

4. What would you do if your friends wanted to play with your pet?
- **a)** Let them play with it.
- **b)** Take it out to show them but wouldn't let them touch it.
- **c)** Snakes and lizards do not like to be handled very much, so say no.

5. Could you feed your pet with dead mice or live insects?
- **a)** Yuck! No way
- **b)** I'd try
- **c)** Yes, no problem

Pet Quiz – Results

If you answered **(c)** to most of the questions, then a lizard or snake could be the pet for you.

Owning a pet: Checklist

All pets need to be treated with respect. Always remember your pet can feel pain and distress— it is not a toy.

To be a good pet owner you should remember these five rules. Your pet must:

- Never suffer from fear and distress
- Never be left to go hungry or thirsty
- Never suffer discomfort
- Always be free from pain, injury, and disease
- Have freedom to show its normal behavior

This means you have to check your pet every day to make sure it has enough water and food, and that its home is at the right temperature.

You must keep its home clean and make sure that your pet has enough room to move around.

You must remember to order new supplies of its food in plenty of time so that it never goes hungry.

If it is sick, you must not let your pet suffer, but take it to a vet to be checked over.

Glossary

aggressive likely to attack or fight

albino white, having no color

arboreal describing animals that spend most of their time in trees

bacteria microorganisms that are found everywhere; some cause disease

blood clotting when blood forms lumps and stops flowing

breeder a person who hatches or rears young animals to sell, such as snakes or lizards

brumation a period of inactivity when reptiles sleep, for example, during cold weather

captive bred an animal that is bred by a person and not taken from the wild

captivity not in the wild

constrictor a snake that crushes its prey with its body

defrosted when a frozen rat is allowed to thaw out to room temperature

dewlap a skin pouch under the throat of some lizards

dislocate to move out of position, to separate

display when an animal shows off to attract a mate or scare an enemy

exotic strange, unusual, from a different part of the world

habitat the place or surroundings in which an animal lives

humid climate a climate with warm temperatures and lots of moisture in the air, often found in tropical forests

lunge move forward quickly

molting when an animal loses or casts off its covering, such as skin, scales, hair, or feathers

musk a smelly, oily liquid produced by some animals

nocturnal describing animals that sleep during the day and are active at night

predators animals that hunt and eat other animals

prey an animal that is hunted by a predator

regurgitate to throw up, bring up food that has been eaten

shed to lose or cast off an outer covering of skin, scales, hair, or feathers

species a group of organisms that have the same appearance, for example, ball python is a species of snake

territorial defending a particular place or area

ultraviolet light a type of light from the sun that we cannot see; this light is needed by many lizards but causes sunburn in humans

venom the poison produced by poisonous snakes

Websites

Click on Reptiles and learn about some different snakes and lizards as well as other reptiles
http://kids.nationalgeographic.com/kids/animals/creaturefeature/

Fun facts about reptiles and amphibians
http://nationalzoo.si.edu/Animals/ReptilesAmphibians/Facts/

A guide for care of lizards and snakes
http://www.animalhospitals-usa.com/reptiles.html

Index

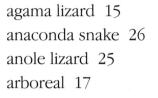